FELLOWSHIP WITH GOD

Life's Great Privilege

MAX D. BARNETT

The Real Purpose of Life Publications

All Scripture quoted is from
the New American Standard Bible (NASB).

The Real Purpose of Life Publications
PO Box 2100
Norman, Oklahoma 73070
(405) 329-2990

ISBN:
978-0-9974519-2-4

TABLE OF CONTENTS

DEDICATION

In deep gratitude to God for making fellowship with Him possible, this booklet is dedicated to:

• **The Glory of God,** who not only makes fellowship with Him possible, but also longs for us to come daily to spend time with Him.

• **The precious family God has given Sandra and me:** Son **Brent**, his wife, **Brenda**, and our four grandchildren, **Blake**, **Katherine**, **Caroline**, and **Brooke.**

• **University of Oklahoma students** by the thousands whom we have tried to help have a special daily time with the Lord and to become disciplemakers.

• **God's people** in many places whom we have tried to help walk with God and to make multiplying disciples.

PREFACE

There is no greater privilege in life than knowing Jesus Christ. The apostle Paul wrote, *"I count all things to be loss in view of the surpassing value of knowing Christ Jesus"* Philippians 3:8. *"In Him are hidden all the treasures of wisdom and knowledge"* Colossians 2:3. Knowing Jesus Christ is the only way to eternal life and the only way to abundant life on this earth.

Spending time in God's Word daily, seeking to know and follow Him, is the greatest privilege of my life. I have found it best to set aside time for this in the early morning before launching into the day. This time with the Lord each day is my highest priority.

This focused time with God is not a burden. I look forward to these special times with the Lord. It is a great joy to pray over God's Word, lift my requests to Him in prayer, listen for His impressions and to fellowship with Him. This time alone with the Lord feeds my desire to be more like Jesus and to be a man God can use for His glory. I am so encouraged to pray as I see the many promises He has made about answers He will give when I will pray aright.

Since the fall of man in the Garden of Eden, nothing is perfect. Our daily time with the Lord will not be perfect. My thoughts sometimes wander when reading the Bible. Then I must go back and read it again, focusing on what I am reading.

Daily I come to worship God and share my life with Him. He is my Lord and if He chooses not to impress something from His Word on my heart that day, I am fine with that. I will be back the next day.

This allotted time only starts my fellowship with the Lord for the day. It launches me out into a day of continued fellowship with Him.

I pray you will join me in having a daily time when you meet alone with the Lord. Make your focused time with the Lord the most important habit of your life. Whatever time is best for you, establish a time daily to focus on your relationship with God by reading His Word and praying.

Guard your time alone with the Lord as a precious treasure, for it is.

Max Barnett
Norman, Oklahoma
2016

CHAPTER ONE

FELLOWSHIP WITH GOD

Relationship Comes Before Fellowship

It is important that we understand God's relationship with man from the very beginning of time. *"Then God said, 'Let Us make man in Our image, according to Our likeness; and let them rule over the fish of the sea and over the birds of the sky and over the cattle and over all the earth, and over every creeping thing that creeps on the earth'"* Genesis 1:26. The word "Us" indicates that the triune God–the Father, Son, and Holy Spirit–conferred together about the creation of man.

The next verse says, *"And God created man in His own image, in the image of God He created him; male and female He created them"* Genesis 1:27. God created the first man and woman, Adam and Eve, and placed them in the Garden of Eden.

"The Lord God commanded the man, saying, 'From any tree of the garden you may eat freely; but from the tree of the knowledge of good and evil you shall not eat, for in the day you eat from it you will surely die'" Genesis 2:16, 17. Satan came along in the form of a serpent bringing his temptation and saying, *"You surely will not die...you will be like God knowing good and evil"* Genesis 3:4, 5.

God indicated that if they ate from the forbidden tree, *"You will surely die."* Satan said, *"You surely will not die."* God said one thing and Satan said the opposite. Now man had a choice to make. Who would he trust and who would he obey?

Adam took Satan's advice and disobeyed God. Adam then died in his spirit; physical death would come later. That day sin entered into the world. *"Therefore, just as through one man sin entered into the world, and death through sin, and so death spread to all men, because all sinned"* Romans 5:12.

Due to Adam's sin of disobedience in the Garden of Eden, fellowship with God was broken and we were all plunged into sin. We inherited our sin nature from

Adam. As a result of sin, each of us is separated from God, dead in our spirit, and incapable of having a personal relationship with God.

The sad truth is that our separation from God, due to sin, can continue for all eternity in the horrible, pain-filled place called hades or hell. Jesus describes what that is like in Luke 16 as he tells the condition of a man after his death. *"And in Hades he lifted up his eyes, being in torment, and saw Abraham far away and Lazarus in his bosom. And he cried out and said, 'Father Abraham, have mercy on me, and send Lazarus so that he may dip the tip of his finger in water and cool off my tongue, for I am in agony in this flame'"* Luke 16:23, 24. Because of our sin, a horrible agonizing eternity separated from God also awaits us.

But along with the bad, there is some good news. *"For as through the one man's disobedience the many were made sinners, even so through the obedience of the One the many will be made righteous"* Romans 5:19. The one man, Jesus, unlike Adam, obeyed God, making deliverance from the bondage of sin and hell possible.

God is holy, just, and righteous, so sin had to be punished. As a result of our sin and God's hatred for sin, we face a severe judgment.

But God from all eternity had a plan to deal with our sin so we would not have to endure hell eternally separated from Him. He would send His own Son to the earth. That Son, Jesus Christ, lived a perfect life and had no sin of His own. Jesus willingly went to the cross where He took the just wrath of God against all sin, our sins, on Himself and paid the penalty for those sins.

A Personal Decision is Essential

It was and is impossible for us to have fellowship with God or to have eternal life with Him due to our sin. But when Jesus Christ, God's perfect Son, died to pay the penalty for our sin, the possibility of our having fellowship with God was opened. God did what was and is necessary for us to have eternal life, but there is something we must do. God provided the "how" of salvation through faith in Jesus Christ, but "who" receives the benefit of what Christ did depends on every person's choice.

Notice in the two verses below how clearly Jesus states what is essential to be able to have eternal life.

"For God so loved the world, that He gave His only begotten Son, that whoever believes in Him shall not perish, but have eternal life" John 3:16.

"He who believes in Him is not judged, he who does not believe has been judged already, because he has not believed in the name of the only begotten Son of God" John 3:18.

Later John writes the following truth: *"He who believes in the Son has eternal life; but he who does not obey the Son will not see life, but the wrath of God abides on him"* John 3:36.

By believing what Jesus Christ did for us on the cross, we will be forgiven by God and eternal life is ours. *"For the wages of sin is death, but the free gift of God is eternal life in Christ Jesus our Lord"* Romans 6:23. By faith in Christ we have forgiveness of sins, eternal life, and the potential of our having fellowship with God.

It was recorded of Jesus, *"Of Him all the prophets bear witness that through*

His name everyone who believes in Him receives forgiveness of sins" Acts 10:43. The Bible says all the prophets testify that everyone who believes in Jesus Christ receives forgiveness of sins. There are many in the world's religions who claim to be prophets. If they do not testify that forgiveness of sin is available only through faith in Jesus Christ, they are false prophets.

By placing our faith in Jesus Christ, we can now have the righteousness of Christ in place of our sin. *"He made Him who knew no sin to be sin on our behalf, so that we might become the righteousness of God in Him"* II Corinthians 5:21. By placing our faith in Christ, His righteousness is then credited to our account.

There is absolutely no other way to be forgiven of our sins, have a relationship with God, and spend eternity with Him in heaven, other than through faith in Jesus Christ. Peter directed by the Holy Spirit said about Jesus Christ, *"And there is salvation in no one else; for there is no other name under heaven that has been given among men by which we must be saved"* Acts 4:12.

There is only one way to be saved and that is through faith in Jesus Christ, the perfect Son of God, Who died on the cross for your sin and rose again three days later. No world religion can save you, as none of their leaders was the perfect Son of God who never sinned and who died on the cross for your sins and rose again.

In speaking to one of His disciples named Thomas, *"Jesus said to him, 'I am the way, and the truth, and the life; no one comes to the Father but through Me'"* John 14:6.

The saying, "There are many roads that lead to God," is false. There is only one way and it is through faith in Jesus Christ, God's perfect Son, Who died for our sins.

If you are willing to turn from your sin, Christ will help you do so as He comes into your life. By trusting Jesus Christ to forgive you and become your Savior, you will be saved and have the life Jesus died to give you. You need to know also that God will be working in your life for the remainder of your life to develop you more and more into the likeness of His Son Jesus.

He promised He would forgive and

save you if you acknowledge your sins, confess Him as Lord, and turn to Him in faith. *"That if you confess with your mouth that Jesus is Lord, and believe in your heart that God raised Him from the dead, you will be saved"* Romans 10:9. *"For whoever will call upon the name of the Lord will be saved"* Romans 10:13.

If you have never made that decision, you can make it now. Regardless of what you have done or how bad you have been, God wants to save you and has made every provision for your salvation. You are the one, and the only one, who can make that decision for you. Right now, will you repent of your sins and ask Christ to forgive you and to become your Savior and Lord?

Once you have made that decision, eternal life is yours. John wrote of Jesus' promise, *"This is the promise which He Himself made to us: eternal life"* I John 2:25. The door to fellowship with God is now open.

Fellowship with God

"God is faithful, through whom you were called into fellowship with His Son, Jesus Christ our Lord" I Corinthians 1:9. God

desires and calls us to have fellowship with Him. Having fellowship with Christ is one of the greatest privileges we will ever have as human beings.

The apostle John wrote, *"What we have seen and heard we proclaim to you also, so that you too may have fellowship with us; and indeed our fellowship is with the Father, and with His Son Jesus Christ"* I John 1:3. As well as having fellowship with God, we need to be a part of a fellowship of local believers. That is what the church was established to be.

God's desire for fellowship with us is not because He has a need. God said, *"If I were hungry, I would not tell you, for the world is Mine, and all it contains"* Psalm 50:12. But God in His graciousness and love desires the very best for us, which is living in union and fellowship with Him.

Once Christ comes into our lives, a new relationship with God begins. *"Therefore if anyone is in Christ, he is a new creature; the old things passed away; behold, new things have come"* II Corinthians 5:17.

Upon becoming a Christian, we are no longer our own, for we belong to God. *"Or do you not know that your body is a temple of the Holy Spirit who is in you, whom you have from God, and that you are not your own? For you have been bought with a price: therefore glorify God in your body"* I Corinthians 6:19, 20.

Christ purchased our lives with His own shed blood. Now notice what He wants with our lives. *"And He died for all, so that they who live might no longer live for themselves, but for Him who died and rose again on their behalf"* II Corinthians 5:15. Christ died for us and rose again and wants us to live for Him.

He does not want us to live for our own pleasure and try to run our own lives. He is the Lord God and wants us to yield to His lordship. *"For to this end Christ died and lived again, that He might be Lord both of the dead and of the living"* Romans 14:9.

When we live for Him, yielded to His lordship, we have an abundant life available to us. Jesus said, *"The thief comes only to steal, and kill, and destroy; I came that they may have life, and have it abundantly"* John 10:10.

Christ is now to be the center of our lives. Paul wrote, *"I have been crucified with Christ; and it is no longer I who live, but Christ lives in me; and the life which I now live in the flesh I live by faith in the Son of God, who loved me and gave Himself up for me"* Galatians 2:20.

Just as we were identified with Adam in sin, now we are identified with Christ in His crucifixion, death, burial, and resurrection. Christ living and reigning in us is life at its best!

Christ now lives in us and we are to live by faith in Him. Paul also spoke of *"Christ, who is our life..."* Colossians 3:4. Paul wrote to the people in Philippi, *"For to me, to live is Christ and to die is gain"* Philippians 1:21. Christ is to rule and reign in our lives, enabling us to live a life of significance, full of meaning and purpose.

The great purpose of our lives becomes to bring honor and glory to our great God. Paul, writing under the leadership of the Holy Spirit, expressed God's desire for us so well when he penned, *"Whether, then, you eat or drink or whatever you do, do all to the glory of God"* I Corinthians 10:31.

Paul made it so clear what was important to him, and it was not treasuring and protecting his own life. *"But I do not consider my life of any account as dear to myself, so that I may finish my course and the ministry which I received from the Lord Jesus, to testify solemnly of the gospel of the grace of God"* Acts 20:24.

God has a desire to use us for His glory and our good. When we become Christians, God gives us spiritual gifts that we may build each other up in the body of Christ and help share the good news about Jesus with the world.

The Holy Spirit has come to indwell those who believe in Jesus Christ. God is now with us to enable us to do what God has commanded us to do and He will never leave us.

Jesus told us what is essential to a fruitful life. *"Abide in Me, and I in you. As the branch cannot bear fruit of itself unless it abides in the vine, so neither can you unless you abide in Me. I am the vine, you are the branches; he who abides in Me and I in him, he bears much fruit, for apart from Me you can do nothing"* John 15:4, 5. Living in dependence upon Him is the way to a meaningful and fruitful life.

After having known Christ as his Savior and Lord for many years, Paul wrote, *"That I may know Him, and the power of His resurrection and the fellowship of His sufferings, being conformed to His death"* Philippians 3:10. Paul longed to know Christ better, and so should we.

Jesus wants us to come to Him daily, even when we are tired, weary, and perhaps discouraged. *"Come to Me, all who are weary and heavy-laden, and I will give you rest. Take My yoke upon you and learn from Me, for I am gentle and humble in heart, and you shall find rest for your souls. For My yoke is easy and My burden is light"* Matthew 11:28-30.

CHAPTER TWO

THE OBJECTIVE OF THE DEVOTIONAL LIFE

Time in fellowship with the Lord in His Word and in prayer should be of highest priority. Some people call their special time with the Lord their Quiet Time, Devotional Time, Bible Reading Time, Conversations with God, or Prayer Time. Call it what you will, but it is that time you spend alone with God in His Word and prayer.

I use the words Quiet Time, Devotional Life, or Devotional Time interchangeably throughout this booklet. The objective of this special time is to have fellowship with the Lord. We do that through earnestly reading the Bible and praying.

Do not lose sight of why you are doing what you are doing. In your Quiet Time you are not disciplining yourself to meet a schedule, or a rule, or trying to earn favor

God. You already have favor with God because of what Jesus Christ did for you on the cross and your acceptance of that magnificent gift. Keep your focus on the Lord and realize the Quiet Time is a method to help you do that. The Quiet Time is not an end in itself. It is like the lens of a camera to help you focus. Remember the focus is the Lord and your relationship with Him.

Jesus was asked by a Pharisee who was a lawyer, *"'Teacher, which is the great commandment in the Law?' And He said to him, 'You shall love the Lord your God with all your heart, and with all your soul, and with all your mind. This is the great and foremost commandment'"* Matthew 22:36-38. That has not changed. That is still God's desire for us.

He wants us to love Him with our whole being. But before that was possible, He loved us. *"In this is love, not that we loved God, but that He loved us and sent His Son to be the propitiation for our sins"* I John 4:10. God loved us so much that He sent His only begotten Son to take care of our sin problem so that we could have a new life and not go into eternal hell due to our sins.

"We love, because He first loved us" I John 4:19. His love for us has made it possible for us to love Him and people.

The daily Quiet Time helps us learn to love Him more. It is not about fulfilling a duty. It is about an undistracted time when God and a weak person love each other and spend time together.

Peter stated a beautiful truth about our relationship with our unseen God. *"And though you have not seen Him, you love Him, and though you do not see Him now, but believe in Him, you greatly rejoice with joy inexpressible and full of glory"* I Peter 1:8.

When Jesus was visiting in the home of the two sisters, Mary and Martha, He commended Mary because she sat at His feet and listened to His words. Martha was anxious about serving and asked Jesus to get Mary to help her. *"But the Lord answered and said to to her, 'Martha, Martha, you are worried and bothered about so many things; but only one thing is necessary, for Mary has chosen the good part, which shall not be taken away from her'"* Luke 10:41, 42 Mary made the wise decision to spend time with Jesus.

A busy missionary once said, “Our Master never asks of us such heavy labor as shall leave us no leisure for sitting at His feet.” If you are working or studying too much, or you are too busy to spend some focused time with the Lord, check your priorities. Maybe they need resetting. Maybe you are more occupied than you should be.

It is essential that we spend time in the Word of God if we really want to know, love, and have fellowship with Him and know His leadership in our lives. God has given us His Word and His Spirit to guide us through life. Remember the Quiet Time is about having personal fellowship with God.

Does it require some discipline to have a Quiet Time regularly? Absolutely. Any great endeavor in life requires discipline. But discipline does not have to be drudgery. I have not found the discipline of a daily Quiet Time to be a burden. Keeping my focus on why I have a Devotional Time helps keep me motivated. I am spending time with the one and only living God Who loves me immensely.

CHAPTER THREE

GOD SPEAKS TO US THROUGH HIS WORD

What we know about God, we primarily learn from the Scriptures. We can have absolute confidence in the integrity of the Bible. It has been painstakingly translated into our language. *"All Scripture is inspired by God and profitable for teaching, for reproof, for correction, for training in righteousness; so that the man of God may be adequate, equipped for every good work"* II Timothy 3:16, 17. The Greek word "inspired" literally means "God breathed." God speaks through the Scriptures to us.

Understanding the context of any passage of Scripture is extremely important for its interpretation. First, we must try to understand the intent of the writer and what the people to whom it was originally written would understand it to mean. Then we can prayerfully seek to understand what

God wants us to learn and do.

God's Word contains both "prescriptive" and "descriptive" information. When the instruction from God is "prescriptive," the choice we have is to obey or disobey. God says, *"You shall not commit adultery"* Exodus 20:14. The Holy Spirit of God also had Paul write, *"Be kind to one another, tender-hearted, forgiving each other, just as God in Christ also has forgiven you"* Ephesians 4:32. In these two passages it is very clear what God said and we have a choice. We can choose to obey or disobey His instructions. There is much in the Scriptures that is prescriptive where God tells us exactly what He wants from us and obedience should follow.

There is also much "descriptive" information in the Bible that describes what is happening in the lives and events of others. Why are the stories of their lives and events recorded?

Two verses in the New Testament help us understand. These tell us how God can use "descriptive" information in our lives. *"For whatever was written in earlier times was written for our instruction, that through perseverance and the encouragement of the Scriptures we might have hope"* Romans 15:4. Another verse much like it says, *"Now these things happened to them as an example, and they were written for our instruction, upon whom the ends of the ages have come"* I Corinthians 10:11. These passages of Scripture can be a great help in understanding what God is saying to us from the lives and events recorded in the Scriptures.

As we read the stories in the Old and New Testaments, we realize these things happened as examples and are written for our instruction. Both the Old and New Testaments contain "descriptive" information.

One day Saul and David were coming back from battle: *"The women sang as they played, and said, 'Saul has slain his thousands, and David his ten thousands"* I Samuel 18:7. What did Saul think about that little song? He hated it because David was credited with being a greater warrior than he.

Why is that story recorded in the Scriptures? Is it so that I will know more about the history of Israel? Yes, but there is far more to it than that. What does God want me to learn from that story? What is God saying to me?

When I read that story, I needed to stop and think. This happened as an example and was written for my instruction. "Lord, what do you want me to learn from this story?" As I reflected on it, I prayed, "Lord, there will be younger men come along who will do a better job than I have done, just as David did a better job than Saul. God, I do not want to be like Saul. I do not want to be jealous of those young men. I want to give my life to helping them."

One day I was reading in II Chronicles 26 and came across the story of what happened with King Uzziah. *"...Hence his fame spread afar, for he was marvelously helped until he was strong. But when he became strong, his heart was so proud that he acted corruptly, and he was unfaithful to the Lord his God..."* II Chronicles 26:15, 16.

What a tremendous warning! When God blesses us and we are recognized for what God has done through us, we must be very careful not to let pride creep in. Notice the Scriptures indicate that Uzziah *"was marvelously helped"* until he was strong. Like Uzziah, we do not become strong without some marvelous help. Uzziah allowed pride into his life which led to his unfaithfulness to the Lord.

Pride is taking credit for what God and others have done in our lives. God hates pride as He so clearly states in His Word. *"The fear of the Lord is to hate evil; Pride and arrogance and the evil way and the perverted mouth, I hate"* Proverbs 8:13.

God also warns us of pride's destructive nature. *"Pride goes before destruction, and a haughty spirit before stumbling"* Proverbs 16:18.

The Bible is very clear that whatever we have comes from God. *"For who regards you as superior? What do you have that you did not receive? And if you did receive it, why do you boast as if you had not received it?"* I Corinthians 4:7. We know God is the source of any good that comes from our lives. *"Every good thing given and every perfect gift is from above, coming down from the Father of lights, with whom there is no variation or shifting shadow"* James 1:17. So I pray against pride and that I will always walk humbly before God.

Remember that what happened in the Scriptures was written for our learning. When we realize that, our time reading the Bible can become very meaningful. As we meditate and pray over the Scriptures, the Word of God comes alive and we begin to hear from God. God can and does become very real to us.

Simply reading a passage of Scripture does not change us. It is only as we think about how we can apply what is applicable to our lives, and do so, that we are changed. Therefore, meditation becomes a crucial part of our Devotional Life. Our goal must be not only information but the transformation of our lives. During our reflecting and thinking on a passage, the Spirit of God can show us what we are to learn and do.

"But prove yourselves doers of the word, and not merely hearers who delude themselves" James 1:22. One of the great problems in the church is that people come and hear a message but often do nothing about it. There is something very deceiving about listening. It is not listening that changes us. It is being obedient to what

we hear that leads to transformation.

CHAPTER FOUR

PRACTICAL SUGGESTIONS FOR THE DEVOTIONAL TIME

Do not wait for a feeling to motivate you to spend time with the Lord. Feelings come and go. If you live solely on your feelings, you will live in defeat.

What the Psalmist prayed is a great place to start when you come to read your Bible: *"Open my eyes, that I may behold wonderful things from your law"* Psalm 119:18.

Select a Time

Set a time each day when it is best for you to have your focused time with the Lord. While a university student, if you are committed to having a daily Quiet Time, you may have it during a break in your class schedule. Time between classes may work well for some as a good time to meet with the Lord. Once you graduate, the likelihood of it becoming an established part of your life is unlikely unless you set a definite time first thing in the morning. If you are a university student, you would be very wise to arise early enough to have a solid Quiet Time before you head into your day.

Unless you get your time with the Lord established in the early morning, you will likely struggle to have a Quiet Time all your life or even quit. Once you are out of school, have a job, a family and other life responsibilities, you will have very limited free time. When you arrive home from work, usually tired, and have a spouse and children needing your time, along with other duties, having a consistent Quiet Time is virtually impossible.

It will be one of the wisest decisions you can ever make to decide to meet with the Lord first thing in the morning. When it is time to get out of bed, get your feet on the floor and never look back. Be decisive. Do whatever you need to do to be awake. When I was a university student and at times not getting enough sleep, I found it helpful to walk around the room reading from the Bible and praying in order to stay awake.

You need to make a decision not to stay up too late. The old saying is true, "You cannot hoot with the owls at night and soar with the eagles in the morning."

Whatever time is best for you should be set aside for this important purpose. There will be times when life demands that you must make an exception from your favorite time for fellowship with the Lord. Vary your time if you have to, but do not miss this special time with the Lover of your soul.

Jesus knew the value of spending the first part of His day with His Father. *"In the early morning, while it was still dark, Jesus got up, left the house, and went away to a secluded place, and was praying there"* Mark 1:35. He also found other times in His busy life to be alone with His Father. It was a habit of His life to seek those times. *"But Jesus Himself would often slip away to the wilderness and pray"* Luke 5:16.

Many of the outstanding Christians through the centuries rose early to meet with the Father. That discipline may also serve you well.

Mothers with young children may find it hard to have the same time daily for their Quiet Time. Taking care of the children God has given you is a God-honoring task and children's needs do not always fit your planned schedule. God knows and understands, so do not feel guilty if you cannot have a "same time" schedule.

Ruth Graham, wife of the famed evangelist Billy Graham, had that difficulty as she tried to rear their five children. So she kept a Bible open on the kitchen table. She would read a verse or small passage as she walked by. Ruth also prayed "on the hoof," as she called it, as she prayed while rushing around doing her duties.

Remember, God is in your life and fellowship with Him is possible at anytime, anywhere. It is said that Susanna Wesley, the mother of John and Charles Wesley and twelve other children, would sometimes pull her apron over her head to shut out distractions so that she could have a special time with the Lord.

Do not develop the attitude that you meet with the Lord once during the day and you are through with God until the next day.

Your Quiet Time, though a specific time to focus on the Lord, should launch you into a day of continued fellowship with Him. It is also legitimate to read the Bible more than once a day.

Paul wrote, *"Pray without ceasing"* I Thessalonians 5:17. The New Testament was originally written primarily in the Greek language. The Greek word translated "without ceasing" does not mean we are to pray constantly. The same Greek word was used to describe a man with a hacking cough. The man does not cough constantly but intermittently.

Sometimes our minds have to concentrate on other things. But our minds should be like a compass. You can shake it and the needle will fluctuate, but when you allow it to become still, the needle will point north. We need to train our unengaged minds to turn to the Lord. Paul wrote, *"We are destroying speculations and every lofty thing raised up against the knowledge of God, we are taking every thought captive to the obedience of Christ"* II Corinthians 10:5. The prophet Isaiah wrote, *"The steadfast of mind You will keep in perfect peace, because he trusts in You"* Isaiah 26:3.

So when our minds are not engaged, they should be trained to turn to the Lord. God wants us to communicate with Him all through the day. We need to share all of life with Him. When we see a beautiful sunset, we can thank Him. Our lives can be so full, because of His presence in our lives, that dozens of times during the day we can turn our hearts to the Lord in worship, praise, thanksgiving, prayer, and intercession for others.

Select a Quiet Place

Find a place that, as much as possible, is free from noise and distractions. That place may change many times in life, depending on your location and circumstances. As a believer, the Lord is always with you, but it helps to have a place and a focused time to especially enjoy time in His Word and talking with Him.

Select a Definite Plan

There are many different plans people can follow in their devotional times. The plan I found so helpful and highly recommend is to read the Bible through each year. That is not so difficult as it may sound. The plan is to read in three different places in the Bible each day. This gives variety. You read in two places in the Old Testament and one in the New Testament. A Bible that gives the historical context of each book is helpful.

Below is how the Bible Reading Calendar begins the first three days of the year (available at the address listed at the beginning of this booklet). The following is an example of the Bible reading plan:

January

1. Genesis 1:1 - 2:3	Job 1:1 - 2:10	Matthew 1
2. Genesis 2:4 - 25	Job 2:11 - 3:26	Matthew 2
3. Genesis 3	Job 4, 5	Matthew 3

I read the passage of Scripture making notes on what I learn and especially what I think God is saying to me in the passages designated for that day. If in the future I want to read any notes I have ever made on Matthew 3, it would have been on or near January 3rd.

Sometimes I write a great deal, sometimes very little, and a few days none at all. I also use my Quiet Time notebook as a journal to record answers to prayer, significant events, and leadings from the Lord.

Monday Jan 1, 2013 Norman, OK
(the day and date) (the place where I am that day)

I make notes on the passages for that day or anything I think God is saying to me. I may also record anything I feel is important in my life. Then I skip a line and begin with the next day.

Tuesday Jan 2, 2013 Norman, OK

I read the passages listed for January 2nd and make my notes.

If God is speaking to me from one of the passages, I want to clearly hear. If my time is limited, I do not feel any urgency to rush on to finish all the reading of the other passages listed for that day. If I do not have time for all the passages, I read the others later that day or the next. The objective is to meet with God, not just read the three passages. Most days there will be no difficulty reading through the three passages during the Quiet Time.

I choose to use a loose leaf notebook so a sheet can be easily removed should I want to share with someone what I have learned. I use a notebook with 4 inch by 5½ inch paper. Some may prefer to use a bound notebook.

At the end of the year I write the year on the spine of the notebook and place it on a shelf. It is very encouraging to go back periodically and read what I have written in past months or years. I can find any note I have made on any passage of Scripture for the past many years by looking at the Bible Reading Calendar and noticing the date I would have read that passage. I can also find the journal notes I have recorded about significant events in my life.

Using this Bible Reading Calendar enables me to read through the Bible in my Quiet Time each year. If God has anything to say to me from any place in the Bible any year, I do not want to miss it. Do I understand everything I read, especially in the Old Testament? Certainly not! But

I often find nuggets and principles that I well understand.

This plan can also be a tremendous help in our ministry to others. Leroy Eims, who served with the Navigators and is now with the Lord, once told me, "If I were in a local ministry, I would try to get everyone following the same plan in their Devotional Time so that they are all reading the same passages each day. As a result, they can share and discuss what they are learning."

If you are a pastor, collegiate minister, youth director, Sunday school teacher, leading a Bible study, a discipleship group, or discipling individuals, I would highly recommend that you and those you lead read the same passages in your Quiet Times. You will experience great benefits as you share with each other what God is saying to you.

It is also a great plan for a married couple to use. My wife and I have our individual Quiet Times reading the same passages and when we meet for breakfast, we often have insights to share with each other. We have fellowship together, uniting our hearts around the Word of God. As a result, there can be much more sharing of the Word together. On occasions we have had our Quiet Times together, but that is not our normal routine.

This plan also holds me accountable. I know exactly where I am to read in His Word each day. As a result, I am able to read through the Bible each year.

This Bible Reading Calendar also allows for flexibility. If you are discipling a new believer or working with young people just starting to have a Quiet Time, you may have them read only the New Testament section. This can prevent them from feeling overwhelmed and also allow some time for growth toward maturity.

For several years, I have read the New Testament section for the day and the day prior, so I read through the New Testament twice in my Quiet Time each year, as well as the Old Testament once. You can vary the plan any way you think best.

As my desire for spending time in fellowship with the Lord grew and I had more unscheduled time, I wanted to read through the Old Testament twice and the New Testament three times in the year. To accomplish this in my Quiet Time, I read the portion for yesterday and today in the Old Testament. In the New Testament, I read the portions two days before, yesterday's portion and then today's. That enabled me to read the Old Testament twice and the New Testament three times during a year. The repetition is also very helpful. I often see things I had not seen a day or two before.

What a phenomenal privilege we have to come to the Lord and have fellowship with our great God! And the primary avenue over which we travel for that to happen is through reading the Bible and praying.

This plan gives some structure that exposes us to all that God has said in His Word. It helps keep us from just wandering around in the Bible or going to our favorite passages.

oops, guilty as charged

CHAPTER FIVE

TOOLS TO HELP

A Bible

If possible, get a Bible with large enough print so you can read for a good period of time without eye strain. There will be times when you will have a desire to read the Bible for a long period of time. A good translation that is as close to the original languages as possible is the best choice. In the English language, a New American Standard or an English Standard Version are good choices. You want a Bible that is a good translation more than a loose or paraphrased version that is more of an interpretation. Some may choose to use another translation and some may use a different translation every year in their Devotional Time.

Bible Reading Calendar

As mentioned earlier, it is available at the

address listed in the front of this booklet.

A Quiet Time Notebook

With paper, a pen, and your Bible, you have what you need for your time alone with the Lord. I have found it helpful to have a notebook that I use for my Quiet Time and things related to my walk with God. A notebook to help in your spiritual life can be a great asset. Some people will use an iPad, an electronic notebook or a computer for reading and note taking during their Quiet Time. Do whatever is best for you.

I find that my pen and notebook allow me great flexibility. I also use my Quiet Time notebook as a journal, thus enabling me to have only one notebook. For many people in the world, a notebook is much easier to attain and afford than an iPad, an electronic notebook, or a computer.

Here is the way I have my notebook set up and it serves me well:

I have found that having **five dividers** are helpful. You may have more tabs if you like.

1. Quiet Time - Keep the Bible Reading Calendar in your notebook. You may want to hole punch it to fit into your notebook to keep it from being separated. Have paper so that you can make notes during your Quiet Time. You can record insights God gives you from His Word. You may also want to write about important events in your life.

2. Prayer - Here is where you keep the list of people and things for whom and for which you want to pray. This will be a changing list as God answers prayer and as you take on other people and interests for which to pray.

3. Scripture Memory - Memorizing verses that God has impressed on your heart during your Quiet Time allows you to long remember what God has said to you. You may find the booklet *The Value of Memorizing Scripture-Treasuring the Word of God* very helpful in how to successfully memorize and retain the Scriptures. It is also available at the address in the front of the booklet.

- **Verses Memorized** - By writing verses you want to memorize on cards and keeping them with you is a great way to have verses available. You can memorize in spare moments, as well as review and meditate on some of those memorized portions of scripture. Keep a list of all the verses you have memorized, in case you lose your verse cards.

- **Future Memory** - Write down the references and the essence of the passage you want to memorize and at a later time you can write them on cards to memorize. You will find verses you want to memorize in your Quiet Time, hear at church, hear at conferences, read in books, and that others share with you.

4. Messages - In your lifetime you will likely hear many messages in church and at conferences. Take notes so that you can later pray over them and be obedient to what God has said to you. *"For this reason we must pay much closer attention to what we have heard, so we do not drift away from it"* Hebrews 2:1.

I usually take a couple of sheets of paper from my notebook and slip them inside my Bible before going to church. I can take notes but do not need to take my notebook.

You can later file your notes by topics or by the book of the Bible from which the message came. I have hundreds of messages filed from sermons I have heard. This provides valuable resources from which to draw. Try to gain all you can from every message you hear. Sometimes I discard the notes, but it helps me learn by taking notes.

I have noticed **four things** about people who do not take notes in church and at conferences:

- Many do not plan to do anything about what they have heard. The truth is that many church attenders are no different from what they were one hundred sermons ago. Just listening does not change you. James 1:22 says, *"But prove yourselves doers of the word, and not merely hearers who delude themselves."* There is something very deceiving about just listening. It is only as you obey what you hear that you are changed. To be changed into the image of Christ is our ultimate goal.

• Many do not have a teachable spirit. They are not eager to learn. Psychologists tell us that within 24 hours we forget about 90 percent of what we hear. What a terrible waste when we do not take notes and try to gain all we can from what God allows us to hear! A disciple by definition is a learner.

• Most do not plan to pass on to anyone else what they have heard. The sad fact is that few people are involved in discipling others. They do not listen with an ear, not only for themselves, but for training others. They disregard what Paul wrote, *"The things which you have heard from me in the presence of many witnesses, entrust these to faithful men who will be able to teach others also"* II Timothy 2:2.

• Many people have never been taught the value of taking notes in church and at conferences. I have often thought that if I had gone to university like most people go to church, I never would have graduated. The professor would lecture and about 5 weeks later give an exam. Had I not taken notes and reviewed them, passing that exam would not have been possible.

5. Miscellaneous - This section can be adapted to meet your needs. It can be used for your schedule, projects you are working on, or any number of things that help you in your walk with Christ. You may want to have a "to do list" to jot down the things you do not want to forget, that crowd into your mind when you are spending time in fellowship with the Lord.

Many people may prefer to use their phones or other technology to help them with their schedule and daily plans. Sometimes I will jot down things for future thought which I am not yet ready to put on my phone for action.

Many Christians have no notebook or plan that would help them in their Christian life. A notebook that meets your needs can be very helpful in your walk with Christ.

CHAPTER SIX

HOW TO HAVE A QUIET TIME

As I recall, it was from the writings of the great preacher, Stephen Olford, that the following helpful steps in having a Quiet Time came to me:

- **Waiting and Confessing** - Do not rush into the presence of the Lord. Take a few moments and quieten your heart. Spend some time worshiping God. Praise Him for the great God He is and thank Him for the things He does. Search your heart. Is there any sin the Holy Spirit brings to your mind you need to confess to God? To "confess" means to "agree with God." God says what you have done is sin and you need to agree with Him that it is sin and tell Him so. *"If we confess our sins, He is faithful and righteous to forgive us our sins and cleanse us from* *all unrighteousness"* I John 1:9. When we confess our sins, it should always be our desire to forsake that sin. *"He who conceals his transgressions will not prosper, but he who confesses and forsakes them will have compassion"* Proverbs 28:13.

• **Reading** - Read His Word, seeking to perceive anything God will say to you.

• **Meditating** - Meditate on what stands out to you. What is God saying to you and what are you to do? Someone has well said, "Meditation is the doorway to application."

• **Recording** - Record thoughts that God has impressed on your mind. Journal what is going on in your life. What is God teaching you?

• **Praying** - Pray about what you have read. As you read the Scripture you will find things to pray about for your own life and for the lives of others. Much of your praying can be praying over the Scriptures. Having a list of people, events, opportunities, and things you feel a need to pray about can also be helpful. You will be encouraged as you see God answering what you have listed and prayed for.

- **Obeying** - Seek to obey what God has impressed upon you.

- **Sharing** - Try to share with another what God has said to you.

I will say it again, "Meeting with the Lord daily in His Word must be of the highest priority." God desires us to come to Him each day to worship and thank Him for all His goodness. *"Bless the Lord, O my soul, and forget none of His benefits"* Psalm 103:2. Gratitude to God should characterize our lives and our time with Him.

SPECK - An acrostic someone shared with me may also help you in seeking to be obedient to what God has said in His Word. It is easily remembered. As you

read a passage you can ask yourself these questions:
Is there …

- **S** a Sin to avoid?
- **P** a Promise to claim?
- **E** an Example to follow or to avoid?
- **C** a Command to obey?
- **K** some Knowledge to gain?

Prayer

God loves us and wants us to bring all our cares to Him. *"Casting all your anxiety upon Him, for He cares for you"* I Peter 5:7. He does not want us to be hesitant to come to Him with our concerns: *"Therefore let us draw near with confidence to the throne of grace so that we may receive mercy and find grace to help in time of need"* Hebrews 4:16. Notice we come to receive mercy so that we do not get what we justly deserve. We also come to receive grace in order to receive what we do not deserve.

He invites us to bring our needs to Him in prayer and not be worried or anxious. *"Be anxious for nothing, but in everything by prayer and supplication with thanksgiving let your requests be made known to God.*

And the peace of God, which surpasses all comprehension, will guard your hearts and your minds in Christ Jesus" Philippians 4:6, 7.

Prayer is such a vital part of the Christian life. I never cease to be amazed at the numerous passages about prayer in the Bible. God has given us so many promises about what He will do if we will pray. Nothing shows our dependence upon God and trust in Him like our prayer life.

• Make a list of people for whom you want to pray. It will be a changing list over time but a great help in keeping you reminded of those God has put on your heart to pray for.

• Pray for your own life. Pray God will do in and through you what He wants. Pray for His leadership in your life.

• Pray for the things that are so important in the Scriptures. Pray for God to thrust out laborers into the harvest, disciplemakers to be raised up, for the spread of the gospel, and other areas of concern.

An Expectant Heart

Come to your special time expecting to meet with God. Remember you are not coming to that time for just what you can get out of it but to worship, speak to, and listen to the Lord. If the Lord does not want to say anything special to you, that is fine. Thank Him, praise Him, and go out trusting Him to lead you in His ways that day.

If we want an intimate relationship with the Lord, we must not neglect our time in His Word. Our Lord spoke to the Pharisees regarding their view of the Scriptures: *"You search the Scriptures because you think that in them you have eternal life; it is these that testify about Me; and you are unwilling to come to Me so that you may have life"* John 5:39, 40. Jesus made it clear that the Scriptures bear witness to Him and He is the source of life. So if we want to know Jesus intimately, we must spend time in His Word, learning about Him and how He wants us to live.

Jesus was being sought by a group of people by the Sea of Galilee. *"Jesus said to them, 'I am the bread of life…'"* John 6:35.

He is the One Who satisfies our spiritual hunger.

God loves for us to set aside time to spend with Him. This should cause us to come with a joyful heart. He wants to have fellowship with us and to transform us more and more into the likeness of His Son. Making yourself available to the Lord day by day through your Quiet Time will yield untold blessings.

Having a daily Quiet Time will be one of the most important and most rewarding decisions you will ever make. Will you decide by God's enabling grace to regularly spend time with the Lord in His Word? The decision is yours. Making the decision to meet in a focused time with the Lord, and doing it, will be one of the greatest blessings of your life.

CHAPTER SEVEN

PROBLEMS YOU WILL FACE

Lack of Desire

There will be times when you will not want to have your Quiet Time. Confess your lack of desire to meet with the Lord and do it anyway. It is challenging to look at some of the Psalms and to see the Psalmists' desire for God.

> *"As the deer pants for the water brooks, so my soul pants for You, O God"* Psalm 42:1.

> *"O God, You art my God; I shall seek You earnestly; My soul thirsts for You, my flesh yearns for You, in a dry and weary land where there is no water"* Psalm 63:1.

> *"Whom have I in heaven but You? And besides You, I desire nothing on earth"* Psalm 73:25.

> *"My soul longed and even yearned for the courts of the Lord; my heart and*

my flesh sing for joy to the living God" Psalm 84:2.

How is your desire for God? Do you long to be alone with the Lord, just to spend time with Him? If your desire to spend time in fellowship with the Lord in His Word and prayer is weak, what can you do? Confess this to God and choose to spend time in the Word and prayer, regardless of how you feel. Feed what little desire you have to meet with God and you will find your desire growing.

Consistency

Making time daily to spend in the Word and prayer will be a challenge. Unless you make a decision that it will be a daily priority, it will not happen. In all areas of life, we have to be disciplined to accomplish what we want. The spiritual life is no different. *"The soul of the sluggard craves and gets nothing, But the soul of the diligent is made fat"* Proverbs 13:4.

Adequate Time

God deserves our best. That is true of

our time. There is nothing we do in life more important than spending focused time with our Lord.

Discouragement

Sometimes we are discouraged and perhaps disappointed because God did not do what we wanted Him to do. Maybe He did not answer our prayers the way we wanted Him to. Maybe we do not think He has answered at all. We must trust that God knows best and believe what He said, *"And we know that God causes all things to work together for good to those who love God, to those who are called according to His purpose"* Romans 8:28. Satan always tries to get us doubting that God really loves us and will do what is best for our lives. Satan wants to discourage us so that we will not have fellowship with our Lord.

If we look at other Christians, we can get discouraged because many of them apparently do not think having a daily Quiet Time is that important. At times we do not seem to be getting anything from our Quiet Time, so we begin to think, "Why do it?"

Sometimes God withholds His

blessing to see whether we will persevere and continue to come to Him, regardless of the immediate results. Persistence is so important and in Luke's gospel, in chapters 11 and 18, Jesus emphasizes the importance of persistence in the area of prayer.

Schedule

Everyone is busy, even if it is doing nothing. You are responsible for scheduling how you live and use your time. Some of your time is given to work, sleep, eating and doing many other things you have to do in life.

You also need to schedule your leisure time, when there is not some other thing you have to be doing. You can have adequate time to meet with the Lord if it is of highest priority for you.

As my friend Greg Frizzell says, "Even when you are busy you still find time to eat." Jesus said, "*...Man shall not live on bread alone, but on every word that proceeds out of the mouth of God*" Matthew 4:4. If you take time to eat, even when busy, you can take time to read the Word of God.

Wandering Thoughts

Sometimes you will be reading in the Bible and suddenly you will realize you cannot remember a thing you have just read because your mind has wandered off to something else. The last time I remember that happening to me was this morning. I have learned to refocus and read the passage again, starting with where my mind disengaged. If your mind turned to something you need to remember or do, make a note so you will not forget and return to concentrating on the Scriptures.

CHAPTER EIGHT

RESOURCES

Do not let anything replace the Bible in your Quiet Time. You want to read directly from the Bible in this special time with the Lord. There are many devotional books available that can be used as supplements to your time in God's Word. A very popular one is Oswald Chambers' *My Utmost for His Highest.*

A great resource which is free to you is the www.discipleshiplibrary.com. Here you will find thousands of messages available on many subjects to help you in your walk with God.

Other available booklets by the author are:
The Value of Memorizing Scripture
The Truth About Calvinism

APPENDICES

I read the first article in the large *Autobiography of George Mueller*. It has since been abridged by someone to remove some of the old English. This first article has appeared in numerous books and other articles, including a very good biography about George Mueller by Roger Steer entitled, *Delighted in God.*

George Mueller trusted God to provide for all the needs for his orphans' homes in Bristol, England, in the mid and late 1800's. When someone would say to George, "You are a man of great faith," he would reply, "No, I am not a man of great faith. I have faith in a great God."

I have included on the following pages two articles about George Mueller which have blessed my life. You may copy these two articles by George Mueller if you would like.

SOUL NOURISHMENT FIRST

FROM THE
AUTOBIOGRAPHY OF
GEORGE MUELLER

"It has pleased the Lord to teach me a truth, the benefit of which I have not lost for more than fourteen years. The point is this: I saw more clearly than ever that the first great and primary business to which I ought to attend every day was to have my soul happy in the Lord. The first thing to be concerned about was not how much I might serve the Lord, or how I might glorify the Lord, but how I might get my soul into a happy state, and how my inner man might be nourished.

"I saw that the most important thing I had to do was to give myself to the reading of the Word of God – not prayer, but the Word of God. And here again, not the simple reading of the Word of God so that it only passes through my mind just as water runs through a pipe, but considering what I read, pondering over it, and applying it to my heart. To meditate on it, that thus my heart might be comforted, encouraged, warned, reproved, instructed. And that thus, by means of the Word of God, while meditating on it, my heart be brought into experiential communion with the Lord.

"I began therefore to meditate on the New Testament from the beginning early in the morning. The first thing I did, after having asked in a few words the Lord's blessing upon His precious Word, was to begin to meditate on the Word of God, searching as it were into every verse to get blessing out of it.

"When we pray, we speak to God. Now, prayer, in order to be continued for any length of time in any other than a formal manner, requires, generally speaking, a measure of strength or godly desire; and the season, therefore, when this exercise of the soul can be most effectively performed is after the inner man has been nourished by meditation on the Word of God, where we find our Father speaking to us, to encourage us, to comfort us, to instruct us, to humble us, to reprove us.

"By the blessing of God, I ascribe to this mode the help and strength which I have had from God to pass in peace through deeper trials, in various ways, than I had ever had before.

"How different, when the soul is refreshed and made happy early in the morning, from what it is when, without spiritual preparation, the service, the trials, and the temptations of the day come upon me!" May 9, 1841

Is reading the Bible a necessary part of your day or does it have a low priority in your life?

George Mueller, after having read the Bible through one hundred times with increasing delight, made this statement: "The most important thing I had to do daily was to give myself to the reading of the Word of God and to meditating on it. I look upon it as a lost day when I have not had a good time over the Word of God. Friends often say, 'I have so much to do, so many people to see, I cannot find time for Scripture study.' Perhaps there are not many who have more to do than I. For more than half a century I have not known one day when I had not more business than I could get through. For 4 years I had annually about 30,000 letters, and most of these have passed through my own hands.

"Then, as a pastor of a church with 1,200 believers, great has been my care. Besides I have had charge of five immense orphanages; also, at my publishing depot, the printing and circulating of millions of tracts, books, and Bibles; but I have always made a rule never to begin work until I have had a good season with God and His Word. The blessing I have received has been wonderful.

"Do you want to know how to meet the problems of the day? Do you want to know what God wants you to do with your life? Then you must pray and consult His wonderful guide book, the Bible, every day.

"If we are too busy to read God's word daily, then one thing is sure – we are too busy!"